THE SEASONS
&
THE WOODMAN

THE SEASONS & THE WOODMAN

A Book for Children written by

D. H. CHAPMAN

with drawings by C. F. TUNNICLIFFE *and an introduction by F. Fraser Darling*

CAMBRIDGE: AT THE UNIVERSITY PRESS, 1941

CAMBRIDGE UNIVERSITY PRESS
Cambridge, New York, Melbourne, Madrid, Cape Town, Singapore,
São Paulo, Delhi, Dubai, Tokyo

Cambridge University Press
The Edinburgh Building, Cambridge CB2 8RU, UK

Published in the United States of America by Cambridge University Press, New York

www.cambridge.org
Information on this title: www.cambridge.org/9780521141420

First published 1941
This digitally printed version 2010

A catalogue record for this publication is available from the British Library

ISBN 978-0-521-04619-0 Hardback
ISBN 978-0-521-14142-0 Paperback

CONTENTS

v

THE GREAT WOOD

Introduction by F. Fraser Darling

WHEN I was a boy I lived near the edge of a great wood. I was between the age of four and five when the unknown depths of the wood began to beckon me inwards, and many years passed before it was all known: even then, perhaps, it held its mysteries. The great wood was all that was left of a still greater forest which covered that part of the country hundreds of years ago. There were enormous oak trees with dense and twisted crowns into which you could climb and hide like King Charles. Some ash trees grew on a damp slope and one of these was hollow and big enough inside for me to make it a little house. I saw many things from there—squirrels rustling among dry beech leaves a little way off, bank voles coming forth shyly at dusk or in the early morning, a sparrow hawk hunting the glade for smaller birds, and once a fox padded all unknowing through the hollow below me. There were birch trees in the wood, rowans, some beeches and sycamores, and there were Spanish chest-

Fox and jays

vi

nuts which someone must have planted among the other trees a hundred years or more before.

The seasons came and went, year in, year out, and the great friendly wood became part of my life. I think I liked spring best because there were so many things coming anew. Each kind of tree came into leaf in its own time and in its own way, some early, some late, some very green and some almost brown at the beginning. And when they were in leaf and the June sun shone down through the canopy I used to watch the different dapplings of shadows below each kind of tree: then looking upwards there were the moving patterns of the leaves in the sparkle of sunlight. Beeches gave such dense shade that the depths of the crown of leaves were all greenness and grey branches: nothing grew below them. Birches seen from below were like a host of dancing dots and rowans made criss-cross patterns of squares and triangles. Late spring brought millions of small caterpillars on to the leaves, some of them hanging from the trees on silken threads, but the willow warblers and wood warblers came also in May and worked incessantly through the summer so that the caterpillars were rarely so plentiful as to make the trees look bare of leaves.

Little streams ran through the wood, high banked and almost hidden by fern. Down there, sitting on a stone in the bed of a stream, I used to watch wrens flitting hither and thither and peeping at me from tangles of tree roots. Once I watched some water shrews playing on a tiny beach of gravel. I shall not forget the first time I found the cross-leaved mossy saxifrage growing by the stream beneath the fern—a common plant surely, but there is a first time to everything.

Autumn did not seem then to be the herald of winter, for the wood took on a new glory as the leaves began to die. Again, each kind of tree turned brown or red or golden in its own way, and all these I knew and loved. I can remember only two years when I could eat the inside of the beech nuts, though I did not know then what Mr Chapman tells you—that the beeches produce good nuts only

vii

once in five years or so. It was in autumn I used to find the Merveille-du-Jour moth resting on the lichened trunk of an oak tree, and now when I see that green-grey lichen on stone or bark I say to myself it is just like the Merveille-du-Jour; how lovely it is.

Winter was tempered in the depths of the kindly wood; harsh winds were less biting and after the snow had fallen it did not drift as on the high moors above, but lay light to take the imprints of tiny feet of bird and beast which had trodden the way before me. Bands of tits and treecreepers flew from tree to tree, working over the bare branches for insects too small for me to see. The wood was a fairyland of real living things, things I knew well though they were not much thought about in the world of houses and school. What I did not know were the many things Mr Chapman has to tell you in this book of how trees are grown and reared and cared for as crops from the land, and of the uses to which men put the different timbers. You, with this book in your hand and the pictures before you, are even more fortunate.

Cone and catkin of spruce

Startled wood pigeons

I. TREES AND TIMBER

THIS book is to be the story of the woodman's year, but since his work is concerned with trees and timber we should do well to discover something about them first of all. Then when it comes to discussing what he does, we shall be better able to see why he does it.

Although there are hundreds of different kinds of trees, distinguished from one another by various details, they all have certain things in common. To begin with, they are all woody plants, and they all consist of three main parts: the root, the stem, and the crown. The root fixes the tree in the soil and drinks in moisture which travels to the other parts; the stem (also called the bole or trunk) is the main body of the tree, supporting the branches; while the crown is made up of the branches, leaves and twigs.

A tree is a living thing, and so in order that it may live and grow it needs to feed and breathe, just as animals must. Its food is in the form of certain minerals present in the soil and certain gases in the air. These foods are absorbed by parts of the tree formed specially for this work, and gradually digested so that they help to make new growth.

The processes by which a tree lives are called *absorption, transpiration, respiration*, and *photosynthesis*. A terrifying thought, but not as bad as it sounds, as we shall see. Absorption takes place through the roots, and transpiration, respiration, and photosynthesis through the leaves and the bark.

The roots of a full-grown tree form a very complicated pattern; you can tell that by looking at an oak overturned by the wind, and seeing how the roots twist and turn, and cut across each other, and throw off other roots from themselves. The older parts have become solid wood, and their duty is to anchor the ever-growing stem and crown to the earth. But for feeding it is the youngest, newest-formed roots that count. Their tips are covered with hair-like growths —the *root hairs*—which take up moisture from the soil containing in weak solution the mineral salts necessary to nourish the tree. This moisture gradually creeps up the stem towards the leaves, where further action takes place, as we shall learn presently. It is hard to say what causes this upward movement, but it is probably a combination of a drawing action by the leaves and a pumping action by the roots.

Now let us leave the roots for a moment and look at the leaves. No matter what kind of leaf we choose—the complicated horse chestnut leaf or the needle-like pine leaf—the obvious feature common to both is their greenness. Leaves of plants are green because of a remarkable green substance to be found in their tissues. This is called *chlorophyll*. It is of the greatest use to plants, as we shall find.

The second likeness between all leaves cannot be seen by the eye alone, but if you can examine a leaf through a microscope you will find that it is dotted with thousands of little holes, called *stomata*. These stomata are used for taking in and giving out gas—in fact, they are rather like nostrils in this respect. One of the gases they take up from the air is called carbon dioxide. This dissolves in the water which the leaves have received from the roots, and is then changed by the green chlorophyll into substances needed as food by the tree—of which sugar and starch are the most valuable.

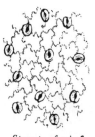

Stomata of a leaf highly magnified

Chlorophyll, so necessary to the life of a plant, is only produced in certain favourable circumstances. Thus, sunlight and a mild temperature are necessary. Sugar, too, can only be formed in the tree under similar conditions. Knowing this, we can begin to understand why many trees are inactive during the winter.

Of the food substances formed, by the action of chlorophyll, from what leaves take from the air and roots take from the soil, sugar is the only one which can be absorbed straight away into the tree itself. In a sense it is the hardest of all to produce; we might regard it as the finished product, as compared with starch, which is only half-way to becoming sugar. The formation of sugar in this way is impossible without bright sunlight, and the process is therefore called *photosynthesis* (from Greek words meaning roughly "produced through the agency of light").

The sugar made in the leaves is in the form of sap, and as such it can flow about the tree to nourish the other parts. There is never any danger of sugar being produced too fast for the tree to digest it, because after a certain limit is reached it turns into starch. Starch is not digestible, but it can be held in reserve, ready to be converted into sugar when required.

You might think that these two movements—the absorption of soil moisture and the circulation of sap—would interfere with each other. This is not so, however, for the soil moisture travels upwards from the roots to the leaves through the outer layers of the actual *wood*, whereas the sugary sap keeps to the inner layers of the *bark*.

The two other processes mentioned earlier were respiration and transpiration, both words suggestive of breathing. You probably know that every time you breathe you take in air (which consists of oxygen and nitrogen), make use of some of the oxygen, and breathe out some carbon dioxide. All plants as living things do the same. This is their *respiration*, and it is done through the stomata of the leaves, and also through little openings, *lenticels*, found in all living parts of the tree. On most trees you cannot see the lenticels clearly, but they show up well in the form of long slits on the bark of the cherry, the hazel and the alder.

Transpiration is the evaporation of surplus water. The soil moisture taken in by the roots contains only a very small amount of minerals, which means that in order to get a sufficient amount of solid food a tree has to drink a great deal of water. Once it has the mineral substances, much of the water that brought them must be got rid of. Transpiration of water takes place through the stomata, and is very active on a hot day.

Alder twig showing lenticels

So much for how a tree feeds and breathes. Let us now see what it is made of and how it grows.

Trees, like all living things, consist of millions of minute *cells*, packed together like the cells of a honeycomb—only many times smaller, of course, and not nearly so regular.

The younger cells are very active and constantly in motion during the growing season. Their greatest activity is that of *cell division*, by which one cell divides itself into two, the two again into four, each of these four into two more, and so on. The newly formed cells grow larger, and this cell-increase is the hidden process behind all the

4

outward changes that we actually see: the growth of the tree and the development of branches, leaves, flowers, and fruit. In time the older cells begin to harden and wear out, and the accumulation of their dead remains becomes the woody part of the tree.

A tree grows in two ways: in height and in girth, or thickness of stem. Height growth is due to the multiplication of cells at the *end* of the branches, where the buds are found. Every year the youngest twigs wake up and stretch themselves out of the buds; then, at the end of the growing season they form new buds, thus protecting the sensitive growing point during the hard wintry weather. Next year new twigs will grow out of these buds, while those which were active before no longer grow in length, but put on thickness.

Terminal leaves of horse chestnut unfolding from the bud

Increase in girth occurs in a zone of cells between wood and bark, known as the *cambium*. It feeds on the sugary sap which flows towards the roots from the leaves. The inner layers of newly formed cells turn into wood and the outer ones into bark. Yet always between the inner and outer layers a thin zone of cambium remains, so that the process can continue year after year.

With a new coat of cells being laid on annually, it is easy to understand how the stem and branches gradually fatten out. It explains, too, why the bark begins to crack after a time, rather like a big man bursting his waistcoat buttons after a heavy meal!

Before going any further, let us get clear what we have learned of a tree so far, as briefly as we can:

1. A tree needs moisture, air, and sunlight in order to live.

2. It is active only in mild or warm weather, and is dormant throughout the winter.

3. Its activities are chiefly the circulation of sap, and growth in height and thickness.

4. Growth is due to the multiplication of cells.

5. In order to multiply, these cells must be constantly fed.

6. Food is derived from the soil, through the roots, in the form of minerals dissolved in water, which are made digestible by the help of gases from the air and sunlight acting on the leaf-chlorophyll.

7. Two channels of moisture are moving at once: (i) soil moisture travels up through the outer layers of wood; (ii) sugary sap travels down through the cambium.

8. As long as it is supplied with sugary sap, the girdle of cambium makes new cells on each side, the inner cells forming new wood and the outer cells new bark.

9. While this is going on new twigs are being formed, also by cell division, so that the crown is putting on height and width in all directions.

10. As the tree grows older the cells nearest the centre gradually harden and die, and turn into timber.

Next time you come across a felled tree or a tree stump in a wood, look at it to see what evidence there is of the tree's method of living and growing. Probably the first thing that will strike you is that it is made up of a series of circles around a core somewhere near the centre.

This core is the *medulla*, or pith, and the circles are called *annual rings*, because one is added every year. They are the layers of wood cells produced on the inner side of the cambium, and you can tell a tree's age by counting the number of annual rings.

Radiating from the medulla, like the spokes of a bicycle wheel, you can sometimes see a number of thin lines, called *medullary rays*. They are not easily seen by the naked eye except in a few species, notably the oak. Only a few of the medullary rays actually join the pith and the bark; the rest begin somewhere across the outer rings and are connected with the bark alone. The purpose of these rays is largely for storing starch; they are a sort of larder upon which the tree can feed when sugar formation slows up because of cold or sunless weather. You can tell that they cut right through the annual rings, because when timber is being dried out, or *seasoned*, cracks are apt to occur in the line of their formation. They can add greatly to the beauty of oak furniture, for if the timber is sawn and worked in the right way the medullary rays produce a type of marking known as "silver grain".

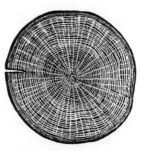

Section through a beech trunk

Another thing you will notice when you look at a tree stool (the stump of a tree left at ground level when a tree has been cut down) or at the butt end of a log is that the inner wood is rather different from the outer—darker in colour, and perhaps less sappy. This is because the older wood nearer the centre has died, whereas there was still some activity in·the cells of the outer rings, which continued to act as moisture channels up to the time the tree was felled. The inner wood—most valuable as timber because it is tough and dry—is called *heartwood*, the rest being *sapwood*. We can prove that heartwood is not necessary to the continued life of a tree by the number of old trees which are completely hollow but continue to put out new leaves year after year, as if they hadn't noticed anything missing inside.

The rim of the stool consists of "bark", which protects the wood from attacks by insects, fungus pests, and the weather; and we know that somewhere between the bark and the wood, although we may not be able to identify it, is that very vital girdle of cells, the cambium.

By the way, do you remember how we said that the upward movement of soil moisture through the sapwood was partly due to a

7

pumping action from the roots? Well, if you look at a newly sawn tree stump cut during the growing season you will see a ring of sap that has oozed out since felling; you may assume that root pressure was responsible at any rate for some of it.

The life story of a tree

Although some trees develop in the first place from offshoots, most of them begin life as seeds. To name a few familiar to us all, there are the acorn, the horse chestnut "conker", the beech nut, the winged "keys" that flutter off the ash in autumn, the little black nut inside the fleshy scarlet berry of the yew; then there are the stones of the cherry, plum, and damson, the pips of the apple, and a hundred more. On the other hand, the cone-bearing trees (pine, fir, larch) produce seeds so small that you may never have noticed them. However, when you consider that there are only about 130 acorns in a pound, whereas the same weight of Scots pine seed numbers 70,000, you needn't reproach yourself for being unobservant!

The structure of a seed can be described quite simply; it consists of an *embryo*, which is the vital germ, surrounded by a store of food to nourish it when it begins to grow. Split open an acorn, and you can see both these parts. The nutty kernel is the food supply, while at the bottom the embryo is visible as a tiny rounded speck.

Before a seed can start to *germinate*, as its first growth is called, certain conditions are necessary; it must have air and moisture, light and warmth. So, because of the last of these conditions, it has to wait until the spring. As soon as the embryo stirs with growth it starts feeding on its reserve supply, and continues to use this until it is sufficiently developed to be able to feed itself direct from the soil and the air. Its first steps are to grow downwards in the form of a root, and upwards in the form of *seed-leaves*, which are of a simpler shape than the usual leaves found later on the particular tree.

8

As the young root lengthens it starts absorbing soil moisture, which travels upwards through the cell tissues into the seed-leaves, where it is acted upon by light and air. You see, therefore, that it doesn't take long for the young tree to get into its normal way of living. Soon, a little shoot forms; this slowly turns into a leaf of the normal shape for that tree, and when it is fully developed it is ready to take on the feeding task of the seed-leaves. Once the change-over is complete, the seed-leaves die off.

The first lot of normal leaves are much harder workers; as soon as they settle down to their job of converting the inner moisture into sugary sap, the seedling begins to grow in earnest. A young girdle

Sycamore seedling, showing first leaves and root

of cambium forms, the roots split up and multiply, and the first stage in the tree's life is over.

Growth slows up as the summer wanes; the sap gradually ceases to rise, and the leaves wither and fall for want of sunlight and warmth. Meanwhile the growing point of the stem has prepared to protect itself by forming a bud, and other buds have appeared in the angle between the leaf-stalks and the stem.

When the following spring brings back the warm weather the seedling comes to life again. The buds open out into new shoots and leaves, and the flow of sap commences once more. During the year a fresh layer of cells is added on either side of the cambium, one to form bark and the other wood; and in the autumn new buds are formed in preparation for the third year.

In later life a new development occurs, for some of the buds turn into flowers. Many of them are quite lovely to look at—cherry, apple, and hawthorn blossom, for instance—whereas others do not display themselves so proudly. The purpose of these flowers is to make fresh seed from which new trees will grow. The method of

making seed from the flower varies greatly according to the kind of tree, but in the most complete cases each flower contains separate male and female parts. The male organs or *stamens* of a flower produce a dust-like substance called *pollen* which, being blown about by the wind or carried by insects, comes into contact with the *stigma*, which is a part of the *pistil* or female organs specially fitted to receive the grains of pollen. The pollen grains are absorbed into the female organs, which then begin to swell and change until at last they contain ripe seeds. In this way the life cycle prepares to turn again—the seed makes a tree and the tree makes seeds—and the seeds are ready for a further generation.

Ash twig with male flowers

Different kinds of trees

There must be nearly two thousand varieties of trees and shrubs to be found in this country, some of them so alike that only experts can tell them apart. But as the woodman is only directly interested in those which are valuable for sale as timber, he may not know more than a score or so.

You can name and recognize trees by the shape of their leaves and how they are attached to the stem; by their flowers and fruits; by the colour and shape of their buds, and their arrangement on the twigs (they may be "opposite", i.e. set in pairs on either side of the twig, or "alternate", i.e. set singly on either side in turn); by their form, or general appearance (you can, for example, tell a Lombardy poplar a mile off!); by their bark, and so on. The best way of learning to spot different trees is to study them at close quarters with the help of one of the many good books on the subject.

We haven't enough room in this book to deal with identification thoroughly, but the following notes will help you to know and name nineteen of the trees with which the woodman has most to do. And at the end of the section I have grouped together the different kinds of timber cut from these English trees, and the chief uses to which each kind of wood is suited.

By the way, there are four terms you always come across in tree books, which are worth mentioning here to avoid confusion. They are: family, genus, species, and variety. An example will illustrate the difference—the Cricket-bat willow. There is a big *family* of trees, called by botanists Salicaceae, which includes the willows and the poplars. "Willow" is the name given to one branch or *genus* of this family, but there are many kinds of willows—it may be a Goat willow or a Crack willow, a Weeping willow, a Pussy willow, a White willow, or an Osier. All these are different *species* of willow. The Cricket-bat willow is a White willow, but with a slight difference. It is not sufficiently different to be given a *specific* name of its own, so it is called a *variety* of White willow. We can tabulate it easily by giving it its world-wide or Latin or botanic name, *Salix alba* var. *caerulea.*

FAMILY	Salicaceae	(Willows, Poplars, etc.)
GENUS	*Salix*	(Willow)
SPECIES	*Salix alba*	(White willow)
VARIETY	*Caerulea*	(Cricket-bat willow)

So next time you play cricket you'll know what you've got in your hand!

One other point to clear the way for our identification of the woodman's trees: of all trees it can be said that they are either

1. *Deciduous* (those which shed their leaves in winter, such as oak, ash, beech, elm); such trees are also sometimes called *broad-leaved* or *hardwood*; or

2. *Evergreen* (bearing leaves all the year round, such as pine, fir, cedar); these are also called *coniferous* (cone bearing) or *softwood*.

There are a few exceptions; for example, in the first group we include the Holm oak, although it is an evergreen, and in the second group we include the larch, although it casts its needles in winter time.

Let us look at the most important *deciduous* trees first:

An oak tree

THE OAK. It almost *had* to come first! Not only is it regarded as our most typically English tree, but it is possibly the most familiar. It is known by its great trunk, supporting a broad sweeping crown, by its lobed leaves, by its thick, furrowed bark—and, of course, by its acorns. Actually there are two species of oak valued for their timber, and you can distinguish them most easily by their acorns and their leaves. They are the Common oak and the Durmast oak. The acorns of the Common oak are produced in groups *on a long stalk* which hangs from the twigs; the acorns of the Durmast oak are set directly on the twigs. Again, the leaf-bases of the Common oak are like a couple of little ear-lobes, while those of the Durmast oak are tapered off.

THE ASH. This tall and graceful tree has a noticeably grey bark, which at first is smooth, but becomes fissured or furrowed as the tree grows older. The leaves are *compound* (each whole leaf consisting of pairs of opposite leaflets set along a middle stalk, capped by a single leaflet at the tip); the edges of the leaflets are toothed irregularly. The buds of ash twigs are opposite, fairly large, and black; a useful thing to remember is that each pair of buds is set at right angles to the pair below or above it.

An elm tree

THE ELM. There are many species of elm, of which two—the Common elm and the Wych elm—are most abundant. They are alike in many ways, and each is quite easy to recognize. The Common elm is tall and upright, and a noble addition to our hedgerows, where it is most frequently found. It grows large branches which persist at no great height from the ground, and very often you can see the main stem through gaps in the crown. The leaves are of a broad, oval shape, with coarsely toothed edges; they are dark green above and

13

a lighter green on the underside, and are covered with rough hairs. The base of the leaf is often lopsided. A disturbing habit of the Common elm is that it is apt to shed its branches without warning; so it is particularly risky to shelter under an elm tree during a storm!

The Wych elm differs in its general appearance by being more spreading than its cousin, and its branches are a little more regular and more drooping. The leaves are much larger, and distinctly uneven or lopsided at the base; also the tip of the leaf is more slender and pointed.

Both species have characteristic fruits, like little sandwiches of parchment with a round lump between.

THE BEECH. Another familiar tree, with a large trunk and a smooth silver-grey bark. The leaves are oval, although bluntly pointed at either end; they are smooth and glossy, with obliquely set straight parallel veins clearly marked upon them. The buds are long and pointed, set alternately (i.e. not opposite each other) on either side of a slender twig. The beech grows best on chalky hills, such as the Chilterns or the South Downs, where it is common in large woodlands and ornamental clumps.

THE HORNBEAM. This is not such a common tree in England, although you will often come across it in the Weald of Sussex, where it thrives on the heavy clay land. It is also found on chalky soils in company with beech—in fact, in some ways it resembles the beech, especially in the leaves. However, the chief features to look for in the leaves are the slender pointed tips, the rough undersides (like the elm leaf), and the double-toothed edges. The dead leaves tend to remain on the tree during the winter; this is very noticeable in hornbeam hedges, which are not uncommon. The buds are plump, brown, and arranged alternately along the twig, to which they are closely pressed. As for the bark, although in young trees it is smooth, it later becomes rough and heavily fluted, and of a dark grey colour. In

14

autumn the easiest way of identifying the hornbeam is by its long tassels of winged nuts.

THE BIRCH. You find the birch growing almost everywhere: in gardens and shrubberies, on commons and hillsides, and in nearly every wood. It is a slender, beautiful tree whose graceful form and delicate network of twigs make it easy to recognize all the year round. The bark is white and papery, peeling off in shreds from time to time. The leaves are tough and glossy, their shape varying from roughly triangular to a tapering oval; they have double-toothed edges and slender stalks. The twigs are thin, and bear short spindle-shaped reddish buds, arranged alter-

A birch tree

nately in spiral fashion. The dark red catkins hang from the twigs all through the winter, which is another point to look for if in doubt.

THE SPANISH CHESTNUT. The Spanish or sweet chestnut is unrelated to the horse chestnut; their names are alike because they both bear chestnuts. The sweet chestnut scores because its nuts are good to eat. It is found chiefly in the southern counties, for it likes warmth. From a distance it looks rather like the oak, but near at hand its differences are clear enough. The bark is deeply channelled in a winding, spiral fashion. The leaves are long and sharply pointed at the tip, with deeply indented parallel side veins and sharp toothed edges. The bluntly pointed reddish buds are arranged alternately on stout twigs. The nuts are dark brown and glossy, pointed, and packed together in twos and threes inside spiky capsules like little rolled-up hedgehogs!

15

THE HORSE CHESTNUT. Most people recognize this in four ways: by the conkers which give such sporting pleasure in autumn, by the rich brown sticky buds, by the upright spikes of pink and white flowers, and by the seven-fingered leaves. Perhaps you are familiar with the yellow or orange scaly bark as well.

THE SYCAMORE. This tree is found at its best on deep, moist soils. It grows in woodlands and hedgerows all over the country, and is not hard to identify. The leaves are *palmate* (like an open hand) with five pointed lobes, the edges being deeply toothed; sometimes they are disfigured by black circular blotches, caused by a fungus. The buds, which are green, are oppositely set on the thick, stiff twigs. During the sycamore's early life the bark is thin and of a pink or purplish colour, but afterwards it becomes grey and roughish, and tends to scale off in slabs. The seeds carry a pair of wings, and they grow in small clusters.

THE WALNUT. Although the walnut produces beautiful and valuable timber it is not much planted in this country. It needs a

Walnut fruit and leaves

deep dry soil and plenty of warm weather to grow successfully; even so, it matures very slowly and cannot be relied on to yield first-class wood. The nuts are the best known feature of the tree; while they are forming and growing they are enclosed in a tough, dark green, fleshy skin, which in time rots away to disclose the wrinkled shell. The leaves are compound, something like those of the

16

ash, about twelve inches long, with anything from five to nine oval leaflets. The leaf-edges are generally smooth, but sometimes they are slightly toothed. If you are in doubt whether such a leaf is a walnut leaf, you should crush it to see if it gives off a strong pleasant smell. The bark is thick and grey, and deeply furrowed in diamond shapes. The buds are a very dark grey, round and hairy, and arranged spirally.

THE HAZEL. You generally come across the hazel in hedgerows and coppices, and more often in bushy form than as a tree. The sweet small nuts make the hazel known to nearly everyone; in a good year the hedgerows will be thick with clusters of "cobnuts" in their ragged green sheaths. The bark is at first of a light yellow-brown colour and of a roughish texture; when older it becomes darker brown and more smooth. The rounded buds are set alternately, and the leaves are oval or rounded with pointed tips and heart-shaped bases. In late autumn clusters of undeveloped catkins appear, which by early spring have become your favourite "lambs' tails".

THE ALDER. This is commonest in wet, low-lying land or along the banks of streams; it rarely grows into a large tree, but more generally assumes a tall bushy form with many stems. The buds are unusual, each one having a distinct stalk; they are brown, and are set spirally along the twigs. Characteristic also are the little woody cones, which remain on the tree all winter. The leaves are rounded, with a tendency to heart-shape, and are toothed at the edges; generally there is a notch instead of a point at the apex. The bark is grey-black and rough.

THE POPLAR. Several species of poplar are grown in England. The easiest to identify is the Lombardy poplar, because of its tall, narrow form and its upright branches. The Lombardy poplar is a variety of the Black poplar, and apart from their shape they have much in common. The leaves of both are roughly triangular with pointed tips and rounded bases, dark green and smooth on either

The black poplar and the Lombardy poplar

side, and round-toothed at the edges; they are attached to the twigs by long, slender stalks which are slightly flattened. In early summer the fluffy red catkins litter the ground at the foot of the tree. The bark is thick, with diagonal furrows, and dark grey, and the buds are large and sticky and sharply pointed. As a tree-shape the black poplar is entirely different from the Lombardy poplar, being very open with down-curving branches.

Other species often seen are the White poplar, which has a smooth grey bark; the Aspen, whose flattened leaf-stalk accounts for the trembling of the leaves usually associated with its name; and the group known as the Balsam poplars, whose leaves give off a fragrant smell.

THE PINES, FIRS, AND LARCHES

The important timber-bearing coniferous trees are few in number, and because, except the larch, they bear their "needles" or leaves all the year round, identification by leaves does not depend on the time of year. If we group them as pines, firs, and larches, and learn the essential differences between these three groups, it will give us a good start off.

The *PINES* bear long needles which grow in *bundles* along the branches. They may be in twos, threes, or fives, according to the

18

species, each bundle being held in a little sheath. Their cones are thick and woody.

The *FIRS* have short flattened needles, set *singly* along the twigs in rows, rather like a comb with teeth on both sides. Their cones are sausage-shaped, made up of many papery scales compressed in layers.

The *LARCHES* have a softer type of needle, growing in *clusters* like little rosettes. In winter the clusters fall to pieces, and the separated needles shower around the foot of the tree. The cones are small, rough and woody.

THE SCOTS PINE. This is the commonest of the pines and the only species native to Britain—all the others have at one time or another been brought over from other countries. You find it most at home on sandy soils, such as heaths and commons, where it flourishes in company with birch, bracken, and heather. The Scots pine has two needles in each cluster; they are fairly short, as pine needles go, and straight. The bark is a good guide, being of a coppery-red colour, especially towards the crown. (Think of the number of Scots people there are with red hair!)

THE CORSICAN PINE also bears its needles in pairs, but they are longer than those of the Scots

A group of Scots pines

19

pine (being up to seven inches) and twisted. It has a pale brown bark which is thick and furrowed on older trees. Another point of difference between these two species of pine is that the lower branches of the Scots pine tend to die off, whereas those of the Corsican do not unless they are growing in close company.

In popular language the word "firs" is applied to three kinds of trees which really belong to different species, although their needles are arranged in the same way. They are the Douglas firs, the Silver firs and the Spruces.

A Douglas fir

THE DOUGLAS FIRS are among the tallest conifers grown in this country. They have large feathery branches growing in whorls— that is, radiating from the stem at the same level, like the spokes of a wheel. The needles are flat, about an inch long, and darker green on top than below. At the tips of the twigs are long, narrow, pointed buds, not unlike those of the beech. In younger trees the bark is smooth and dotted with blisters; if you burst these blisters a pleasant-smelling resin oozes out. Sticking out from the cone-scales are the three-pronged *bracts* which are the wings of the minute seeds ripening inside; this is typical of the Douglas firs.

THE SILVER FIR. In recent years the Silver fir has been planted very little because of the danger to it from disease and frost, but there are still many to be found, grown either for timber or as ornamental trees. The bark of the young trees is silvery grey, but it turns darker as it becomes older. The needles are quite flat, with a little notch at the tip; underneath they are silvery white, which accounts for the tree's name.

THE SPRUCE. Before going any further I would like to bring in the spruces, because they are rather like the Silver firs, and to compare them together now will help to identify them both. Spruce needles are four-sided and end in a sharp point. If you pull them off the twig, or if you look at a dead twig from which the leaves have fallen, you will find that a little peg has been left behind—this happens in no other conifer. On the other hand, if you pull off a Silver fir needle a tiny piece of bark always comes away with it, leaving a circular scar on the twig. The cones on the two trees behave very differently too: Silver fir cones are upright, like candles set on the branches, and when they fall to pieces a spike is left remaining. Spruce cones hang downwards, and when they are ripe they fall off as a whole without scattering the scales.

Two species of spruce are commonly grown in our woodlands, the Common or Norway spruce and the Sitka spruce. The Common spruce has a reddish brown bark which in later years develops in the form of round scales, which peel off from time to time. Its form is familiar enough as the Christmas tree. The Sitka spruce is like it, but it has longer, sharper leaves, green on one side and silver on the other. If you are in doubt as to whether a particular spruce is one or the other, get a friend to grasp a twig. If he merely winces, it's a Norway; if he yells, it's a Sitka!

THE LARCHES. These are the most graceful of the common conifers. We already know two of their characters, the arrangement of the leaves in rosettes, and their unusual habit—for a conifer—of shedding them in autumn. As though to make up for this the larch is one of the first trees to grow new leaves in the spring. They are of a brilliant emerald-green colour, and these along with its small red flowers make the larch tree in spring very pretty indeed. The cones are small and woody, and quite easy to recognize.

The two species generally cultivated are the European or Common larch and the Japanese larch. The branches of the Japanese are reddish brown in colour, in contrast with the yellowish grey of the other, and the leaves have two white bands on the underside.

A larch tree

Timber and its uses

We have learned that wood consists of an accumulation of dead cells. Now although in all kinds of trees these wood cells are made in the same way, you will find big differences between them—not only in comparing one sort of wood with another, but between two pieces of wood of the same species. The quality of timber (that is to say its hardness, colour, strength, lasting powers, and so on) depends much on how a tree has grown. For instance, if you plant an ash in rich, moist, loamy soil it will grow quicker than one put in a heavy clay. It thrives in such a situation, finding all the food it needs, and produces more and larger cells than the other would. The result is a lighter, more elastic timber, such as is needed by the makers of tennis racquets.

Many years of experience have shown timber craftsmen the purposes for which various timbers are best suited. Looking at it another way, for each job they tackle they know what is the best kind of timber to buy. The timber merchant, whose business is to buy trees and convert them into timber in his sawmills for selling to the men who actually use it, may therefore do business with the woodman in two ways. He may either buy a whole crop of mixed trees and take them into stock to be sold when needed; or he may purchase only selected trees of one species for a special purpose.

In the last section we dealt with the trees the woodman grows; here, then, are the uses to which they are put. Some of them, you will notice, don't produce "timber" in the usual sense of the word —or even if they normally would, they are cut down before reaching timber size. This is because they are better suited to other needs; it may be for faggots, or for peasticks, or for hop-poles, or for rustic work for the garden.

OAK timber, like the tree itself, is one of the best known. It is hard and durable, with a straight grain, and is used for structural work in buildings, furniture-making, window-frames, gateposts, carving—in fact, in almost every kind of work where these two qualities of hardness and durability are required. Apart from timber, oak bark is ideal for tanning a specially hard kind of leather, although nowadays cheaper substitutes are often used.

A fifteenth-century oak carving

23

ASH yields a tough and elastic timber, and here again its uses are abundant. Its suitability for tennis racquets has already been mentioned; in the same category we might include billiard cues and gymnastic apparatus (such as parallel bars). Ash is also used in aeroplane building, where its relatively light weight is an added advantage, and in making oars and rudders for boats, and so on.

ELM wood is hard and moderately lasting, the Common elm being rather better than the Wych elm. It doesn't splinter easily; this makes it useful for the bottom boards of waggons and railway trucks, which might otherwise suffer from the scraping of shovels and the constant friction of the goods they carry. Butcher's blocks, too, are generally made of elm—and so are coffins. In building work you come across it in the form of "weather-boarding", over-lapping planks nailed along the outer framework of farm buildings. Elm is also suitable for under-water construction, such as bridge piles, since it resists the decaying effect of water much better than other timbers.

BEECH is another hard timber, but it is rather brittle. It makes good chairs of the cheaper kind, and is valued by furniture-makers because it can be turned on the lathe; it may also be steamed and bent to all sorts of shapes. Street paving blocks, rollers, brush backs, bobbins, and boot-trees are usually made of beech.

HORNBEAM has a white timber of a fine texture. It makes agricultural implements, pulley blocks, and cogs for wooden wheels, such as those you find in wind- and water-mills.

BIRCH timber is firm and quite hard, of a white colour. It is suitable for furniture, veneer, brooms, and clogs or wooden shoes.

SPANISH CHESTNUT is similar to oak, and can be used in many cases instead of oak, for interior work in houses, furniture, fences and gate-posts. Hop-poles are usually chestnut.

HORSE CHESTNUT timber is very soft, and of little value, but it is much used for fencing poles.

SYCAMORE makes furniture, boxes, rollers, dairy utensils (such as churns), and other things that need a hard wood. It is white and close-grained and can be "turned" on the lathe.

WALNUT timber is very valuable, if of good quality, because of its hardness and attractive appearance. It is much used for cabinet-making, veneer and carving, and the best gun stocks are carved out of walnut.

HAZEL wood is useful for hurdles, walking-sticks, and such small purposes. Closely packed bundles of hazel rods are used in the Navy for fenders to protect the sides of ships, hazel being a tough and fibrous wood.

POPLAR produces a soft white timber, ideal for pulp and matches. It is sometimes cut up into boards for cart-making, and for packing-cases.

The *CONIFERS* yield a coarser type of wood, poor to look at in comparison with most hardwoods. Larch is one of the most durable; it makes telegraph posts, masts, railway sleepers, fencing stakes, and pitwood. Scots pine timber, known as "red deal", is used for much the same

Making hurdles of hazel

purposes as larch, but it does not last as long. Scaffold poles are often made of Scots pine. Corsican and Austrian pine are also substitutes for larch, but their timber is coarser and less lasting even than Scots.

SPRUCE is the familiar "white deal". In house-building it appears as rafters and boarding; it also makes scaffolding and ladders, packing-cases, wood pulp, and toys. Silver fir ("white pine") has most of the same uses.

DOUGLAS FIR can be used instead of larch for posts, sleepers, bridges and so forth, but it is an inferior timber in nearly every way.

II. THE FOREST

TO the rambler a forest is merely a delightful place to walk in; delightful because of its wild life and colour, its sounds and smells, and in the way it reveals its character little by little. But the woodman sees more in it than this. The forest is to him what the cornfield is to the farmer—a source of profit and the means of livelihood. There is, then, a great difference between exploring a wood for pleasure and regarding it through the eyes of a woodman. So, for a change, let us put ourselves in the woodman's place.

Now although when you think of "a wood" you probably visualize an unplanned jumble of trees, relieved by occasional clearings and carpeted with all sorts of wild flowers, on thinking over the various woods you have visited you probably recollect distinct differences between them. Most marked, perhaps, is the contrast

A mixed wood

between pine or fir woods, dark and rather forbidding within, and the friendlier, more "natural" woods of oak, ash, and beech. Yet each of these kinds falls into several types, according to the "system" under which the forester is treating them. For, as we shall see when we tell of the woodman's work, every forest that is being exploited for its timber needs to be kept under control. Perhaps it will come as a surprise to you to learn that a seemingly "wild" forest is not as wild as it looks. Of course, in some woods it is clear at once that they have been artificially planted; you can tell that by the way the trees are set in straight rows. But even those that look as if they had been growing of their own accord for hundreds of years may nevertheless be sternly controlled by the forester who is tending them.

One way of describing the character of a wood is to classify it as *pure* or *mixed*. A pure wood consists of trees of one kind only, such as a beech wood, or a larch wood, or a hazel coppice. A mixed wood contains more than one species; most of the wilder-looking woods are made up of all sorts of trees—oak, ash, sycamore, beech, and a dozen others. Some *planted* woods are on purpose stocked with a mixture, such as larch with beech, so that each can help the other to grow.

The "systems" mentioned above are the various methods of treating the woodland crop. There are three systems: *high forest, coppice,* and *coppice-with-standards.* When a forester talks of high forest he means a wood containing trees which have grown up from seeds, sown either naturally or by hand. Pine woods are high forest, so are beech woods—in fact, most woods are grown under this system. You will understand more fully what it means when you compare it with the other two systems.

A coppice is a wood consisting of shoots which have sprung up from the stools of felled trees. Some kinds of trees make coppice very easily; with conifers, on the other hand, coppice is impossible. In practice only a few species—in particular hazel, Spanish chestnut, and osier—are treated in this way, and then only for special purposes. Coppice shoots are never encouraged to grow for more than about fifteen years, which means that they don't reach timber size. Instead, they are used for such things as peasticks, split fencing-pales, stakes, etc.

Coppice-with-standards is a combination of the other two systems. Such a wood contains a number of maturing trees ("standards") growing farther apart than they would be under high forest conditions, surrounded by an underwood of coppice shoots. The advantage is, of course, that you get both large and small produce from the same wood.

What about making an imaginary tour of the woodlands on a big estate, not just for exercise but to see them as the woodman does? I know the very place, right on a spur of the Downs, where the chalk is overlaid by a soil of clay with flints and the hillsides contrast strongly with the more fertile valley bottoms. I advise you to wear the oldest clothes you have ever imagined, and the toughest shoes you can think of!

First of all we'll visit Greendene Wood, the largest and loveliest of them all.

28

Greendene Wood. This, as you notice, is practically a "pure" wood, since nine-tenths of the trees are beeches. The remainder are sycamore, cherry, ash, and an elm or two. They seem to be of all ages, some fully mature, others younger and more spindly, while here and there are patches of seedlings grouped round the bigger stems. The whole appearance of Greendene Wood suggests that it has sprung up naturally, as indeed it has. Beech grows at its best on soil and in a land of this type: it loves the chalk, and asks for nothing better than the gentle slopes where water cannot stagnate round the roots and frost is dispelled early in the winter day.

A "pure" wood of beech

Not many miles from here is a district where furniture is made—chiefly the cheaper, more practical sort—and for many years now Greendene Wood has supplied timber to the same firm of manufacturers. Their buyer knows from experience the quality of timber Greendene can produce, and he will tell you how his father before him used to come over yearly for the same purpose. So as long as beech continues in demand, what better than that it should be grown here where it is known to thrive?

The wood is managed according to a policy called the *selection system*. Every year or so the forester goes carefully through the whole stand and marks those stems which are ripe for felling—the veterans of eighty years and more. He must not be too generous, otherwise he will exhaust the resources of the wood too soon. The "selected" stems are felled and removed to the buyer's yard. Meanwhile the other trees are growing towards maturity. In the distant future the seedlings we see now will suffer the same end, but by that time they will have given rise to new generations of beeches. In this country beech happens to be one of the few trees that will plant itself successfully. Therefore in Greendene Wood where trees have been felled there is no need to plant up the gaps with stock grown in the nursery; Nature will do that of her own accord, and save a lot of

A grey squirrel

trouble! Good seed years don't come every autumn, but every five years or so the beech produces a bumper crop of "mast", and in the spring the seedlings pop up thick and fast.

These cherries we occasionally pass are of little value as timber, but the woodman has left them alone until now they are of impressive size; they, too, are self-seeded. The sycamores can often be sold along with a "parcel" of beech; they are not valuable enough to be sold by themselves these days, but there is an occasional demand for them, and timber merchants as a whole do not mind buying them in small numbers.

Do I hear you asking what causes the sort of woolly blanket you find on some of the beech trunks? Well, it's due to a small insect called the *felted beech coccus*. It's a poor creature, and seems to us to live an aimless life. As it has no legs it can't move about, but spends its days attached to the bark by little tubes situated where its mouth ought to be: through these tubes it sucks juices from the beech bark —and that is about all it seems to do to keep itself occupied! Thousands of the insects accumulate in colonies, and as a protection against the weather they exude this felt-like substance, which forms a white mass on the trunk.

And, talking of pests, I just heard you admiring one: the furtive grey squirrel that shot across our path and vanished into the branches of the crooked beech behind us! The woodman is his sworn enemy, and not without cause, for the squirrel lives on fruits, seeds, buds, and young shoots; moreover, he will often spoil young trees beyond recovery by nibbling round the bark. The grey squirrel, by the way, is really more of a rat. He doesn't belong to this country like his more handsome cousin the brown squirrel; and sad to say the two animals don't get on at all well together, and the native is gradually being ousted by the visitor.

I daresay you have been wondering what is the good of preserving some of the miserable-looking beech that show up so badly beside their healthier neighbours. It is clear that the very twisted ones will never grow into anything likely to yield the straight timber the buyers want; so why doesn't the woodman comb them out, cut them down, and have a good spring clean? The answer is that such trees, although not marketable, may very well be useful to the woodland crop as a whole. Two things essential to a forest are—as the forester puts it—an even canopy and a clean floor. An even canopy requires that the crowns of adjoining trees should be close together, and a clean floor means that the ground should be clear of weeds and useless undergrowth. If the woodman were to cut out all the scallywags at once there would be a gap in the canopy caused by the removal of their foliage. In would come the sunlight, and up would

31

pop the weeds, which were only waiting for such a chance as this to compete with the trees in the struggle for air, light, and soil moisture. Another effect would be to encourage the remaining trees to waste their energy in growing side branches, whereas the woodman wants them to keep shooting upwards so that they develop a long, clean stem. Therefore the poorer specimens are allowed to remain until their removal would cause no serious shock to the canopy as a whole.

I see you are interested in that old trench, nearly filled in with chalk and dead leaves. There are four of them in Greendene Wood, and once upon a time they were sawpits. In these days, when a tree is to be cut into planks it is laid on a movable bench and fed into a rapidly revolving circular saw. But before the days of machine power all planks had to be cut by hand, and the manner of doing it was this. Two men were employed, the more important being the "top-sawyer" and the other the "bottom-sawyer". They worked at a rect-angular pit, dug to a depth of five or six feet, and generally lined with bricks to make it more permanent. The tree butt, neatly trimmed of branches and cross-cut at either end, was laid on top of the pit and secured on cross-pieces. It was then the business of the sawyers to saw the butt into planks of the requisite size, using a long two-handled saw in an up-and-down movement. The top-sawyer's re-sponsibility was to see that the saw didn't deviate from the given line; all the time he would take the main pull of the upward thrust.

32

Sawing a tree into planks at the pit

As for the bottom-sawyer—well, have you read what George Sturt says about it in his intensely interesting book *The Wheelwright's Shop*? Mr Sturt wrote from experience: "One got a queer glimpse of the top-sawyer, as one glanced up (with puckered eyelids) through the falling sawdust. Gradually the dust accumulated about one's feet, and eventually it had to be shovelled up into sacks....I never had confidence enough, or muscle enough, to choose the top-sawyer's arduous post: I was only bottom-sawyer. And truly the work was hard enough there, though I suspect I didn't do my share. I suspect so, judging from the frequency of the top-sawyer's exhortations to 'Chuck her up'. (Pit-saws are always feminine.) How was a man to chuck her up when his back was one ache and all he could do for rest was to lean his weight on the handles of the saw-box for the down-pull? When the down-streaming sawdust caked on his sweaty arms and face?...Not but there were compensations, at least for the bottom man. He might not, indeed, quite go to sleep. He had to keep the saw perpendicular, to 'watch the cut' as best he could through the ever-descending sawdust, and now and again he halted (straightening his back) to carry out the blessed command from the top-sawyer to drive in a wedge or to 'oil-up'. But with these exceptions the bottom-sawyer's work was placid in the extreme. The work was hard enough to prevent thought, there was nothing to see beyond the brick walls of the saw-pit, and the up-and-down sway of arms and body was frequent and regular enough to induce a restful drowsiness."

Most sawpits were established in the yards of timber merchants and other users of wood, but sometimes a tree was too big to be hauled out of the wood, so that a pit had to be dug on the spot. That is why their remains are not uncommon.

Reeve's Copse. The next wood we visit is of a different character from Greendene. It lies in the valley where the soil is deep and

Hazel coppice

rather heavy, and is called Reeve's Copse. It is stocked with hazel coppice, each tree comprising several shoots growing from a low stool. Here and there we find an ash or an oak, most of them reaching maturity. Do you observe that the coppice shoots are in various stages of growth, some being about fifteen feet high and others only a couple of feet or so? And also that the height classes seem to fall into well-defined groups? This is, of course, because the Copse is cut on a regular rotation. It is about thirty acres in extent, and worked on a twelve-year system, so that every year the woodman cuts over a block of two and a half acres. It is very easy labour, as he can sever each shoot with one or two clean cuts of his bill-hook; he leaves the stools intact to grow yet another crop of shoots. There is a good local trade for these poles. Most of the villagers are regular customers; they use the larger shoots for training peas in their gardens, and the smaller ones for fire lighting. A certain quantity is required by the hurdle-maker who lives in the next village. The woodman makes these shoots up into bundles, which he fastens strongly with wire; the bundles are known hereabouts as "bavins".

As each block of coppice reaches its turn to be cut, the "standards" —those few oak and ash which remain—will be felled and sold; but since the system of coppice-with-standards doesn't pay very well, they won't be replaced. Before long the hazel shoots may not be worth growing; the market isn't a very profitable one even now. When that time comes, Reeve's Copse will lose its present character, and I daresay a crop of larch will be planted.

Park Covert. The last wood we shall have time to visit—Park Covert—is in process of gradual transformation from hardwood to softwood. Coming to it from the south side it looks a grand mixture: oak and ash, beech and sycamore, a Wych elm or two, a Silver fir, a hornbeam, two poplars and a crab-apple...what a place to learn the different species! But—a word in your ear—the forester isn't very proud of Park Covert! It's a mess, and that worries him because it takes so long to tidy up. The trouble is that it has been neglected for so long that it has got out of hand. Do you notice how little good as timber trees most of them are? Look at those twisted stems, and the rough branches, and the irregular crowns. And those great gaps where we have to make a wide way round to avoid the brambles. There isn't more than one tree in four any timber merchant would look at. So what the forester has to do is to clear fell a portion every year, use the trees as best he can—selling those that are saleable, and cutting up the rest for firewood and fencing-stakes—and replant the felled areas with some profitable species. He can't cut down the whole wood at once, because apart from anything else he hasn't enough men to help him, which means that a gradual reconstruction is the only solution.

And here, near the middle of the wood, enclosed in wire netting to keep out the rabbits, is the group he planted last, a plantation of Douglas fir. They ought to grow well here; there's plenty of shelter from winds, the ground is high enough to be fairly free of lingering frosts, and the surrounding part of the old crop isn't too thick to steal the light from the young firs. They look insignificant enough now, it must be admitted, but in a few years they will have grown high enough to conceal you or me.

Young Douglas firs

In the next clearing we find a growth of larch, with an occasional row of birch. I daresay the birch is introduced purely to help the other; it is a good "nurse" and protects the larch during the early frost-tender stages. When the larch is well established the birch will be removed, with perhaps a kindly thought of gratitude for its help and regrets that it couldn't stay longer!

Near the edge of Park Covert there is a plantation of Scots pine. A seam of poor, sandy soil is known to exist here, and the more "exacting" species won't grow. Once more you notice the whole block is protected with netting: it's an expensive addition to the cost of planting, but it has to be done, otherwise rabbits would soon damage or kill most of the young plants.

III. THE WOODMAN AND
HIS WORK

FROM what you have read so far, you will already have gathered something of what the woodman does, and our recent visit to the forest has given us a preliminary idea of his work. You may be wondering if there is any difference between a woodman and a forester. Well, strictly speaking, there is. It is very much the same as the difference between the farm labourer and the farmer. That is to say, the forester is the man in charge of the woodland operations, and although on small estates he may do the actual work just the same as his men, in other cases his time will be fully occupied in general supervision and management.

The forester, like the farmer, derives his living from the land; but whereas the farmer uses the land for growing food, the forester uses his for the production of timber. By this time you will know that this isn't merely a question, as some people seem to imagine, of visiting the nearest wood and felling as many trees as are required. The amount of timber in any country is limited in quantity—in Britain, for example, the stock isn't nearly as much as we should like. Therefore the forester has to replant where he has felled, and very often new areas of rough land are taken in hand for the creation of "artificial" forests.

Now although woodlands serve other purposes—such as game cover, shelter, or ornament—the forester's business is to turn them into good saleable timber. None of us likes to see a beautiful old wood cut down, yet this is only the same sort of process, though on a larger scale, as harvesting corn. We don't condemn the farmer when

37

we see his wheat falling before the harvester; we accept it as natural and proper. And we know that much as we enjoy the sight of a field of ripe grain, if it isn't cut in due season it will rot away and become wasted. The same is true of a forest. The time comes when it is ripe for felling; and to leave it standing after that means that it will gradually get worse, until a day comes when it is fit for nothing but firewood.

The forester, then, grows timber for a living, and in order that he may make as good a living as possible he wants to produce the best quality timber in the shortest possible time. That is an important point. He has only a limited area of land to work on, and if by his skill he can grow an equally saleable crop in ten years less than his neighbour can, then he is that much better off. He can fell and sell his trees, plant afresh, and when his neighbour is only thinking of sending for the timber merchant he will already have a ten-year-old plantation established. Oh yes; there is a great deal to learn about the wise management of timber; the business of growing trees isn't just a matter of sowing a few acorns and bequeathing the result to one's great-grandson! In fact, forestry is already a highly developed science; scores of books are still being written about it, and our knowledge of forestry is growing all the time as the various research departments make some new discovery: how to prevent such and such disease (and a tree has so many enemies that it is almost a wonder it ever manages to keep alive), how to improve this bit of land so that trees will grow better on it, how to reduce the expenses of this or that operation, and so on. All this with one end in view: the economical production of timber; for there is no need to tell you that wood with its thousand uses is one of our first necessities still.

During the course of the year the woodman, who probably has charge of trees in all stages of development, may be engaged in any of the hundred-and-one processes which timber growing calls for. But it will be simplest here to relate how a tree is "produced" from the beginning, because although not every forester starts from the beginning (some preferring to buy their young plants "ready made"), a great many do raise their stock from seed.

The Tree Nursery. First, then, there will be a bit of land set aside as a nursery. It need not be very big—something like one-twentieth of the woodland area to be planted each year will suffice; but for all that it will need constant and careful looking after. The nursery will be divided into small plots, of which one will be the seed-bed. The forester will probably buy his seed from a dealer; unless he is planting on a very large scale he won't rely on what he can gather from his own woods. The larger seeds, such as acorns and beech-mast, may be worth collecting, but the seeds of the coniferous trees, which are so largely grown to-day, have to be extracted from their cones, and this is a job by itself.

The soil of the seed-bed needs to be most highly cultivated and brought to the finest possible tilth, in the same way as an onion bed. The seed is sown in rows, and in a few months there appears a crop of *seedlings*, so minute and so delicate that it is a wonder to believe

39

Weeding the seed-beds

that one day some of them will grow to a height of fifty feet and more.

The next step is to lift the seedlings, destroy those which are weak or badly formed, and *line out* the rest. This is usually done when the seedlings are two years old, but sometimes after the first season. The object of transplanting is to give each plant more room to grow than it had in the seed-bed; this enables them to form bushy fibrous roots, and when growing trees a healthy root system is half the battle.

The young plants, now known as *transplants*, remain in the nursery lines for a year or two, when they are either taken direct to the plantation itself or transplanted for a second time in order to develop still more before being moved into their permanent home. Descriptions are given to young trees according to the number of years they have been in the seed-bed and in the nursery lines. Thus a *two year one* plant is one which has spent two years as a seedling and one as a transplant; and one which was two years in the seed-bed, followed by two years in the nursery lines, and transplanted again for a further year is described as "2 yr. 2 yr. 1 yr."

At last the transplants are ready for setting out in the plantation, and we shall see later how this is done. But because, for various reasons, they are planted close together a good many—in fact, the larger proportion—will be intentionally removed in a few years time. This is a selective process known as *thinning*, and one which is most important to the welfare of the wood as a whole. Pruning, that is to

40

say the removal of the lower branches, is also necessary in many cases; and I nearly forgot to mention weeding, which sounds a fiddling sort of thing in connection with so large an object as a forest. But weeding is only necessary until the young trees have overcome the various wild plants that spring up to compete with them.

There is one aspect of the forester's work which appears to be discouraging: that is, unless he happens to be a very young man and is growing timber on a *short rotation* he cannot hope to see his work come to maturity. Certainly this can be a rather depressing fact. You may hear a woodland owner say, "What's the use of my planting oaks here? It'll cost me a lot of money, and I won't live long enough to derive any benefit from it." Quite so; we can understand his attitude. Yet the mature forests from which he now gets his profit and enjoyment were planted not by him, but by his forefathers; they are a sort of heritage, and if he looks at them in that light he will continue to keep them going by replanting where he has felled. Of course, it is for this reason that a government department or some corporate landowning body, such as a college, is well suited to the continued propagation of our forests. They do not die as persons do, nor do they need to work for immediate profits. The Forestry Commission, for example, is gradually creating a large number of state forests, which in time will do much to lessen England's dependence on timber from other lands. Their forests (or we might say "our

An afforestation landscape

forests" since they are a national possession) are for the most part still young and growing, and will remain so for many years to come, but in course of time, because of what the Commissioners are now tending and planting, we shall be the owners of large rich new forests —a source of valuable timber, and a delightful addition to our scenery.

One other question may be considered here: How does the wood-man know what to do next? Surely, you may think, if you are trying to produce a crop which will be growing for forty or even a hundred years, you must have some idea of its future treatment, some guide as to what you are aiming at, and some record of what has been done already—if only for the guidance of those who may take over the management later on. The answer is that the forester, before setting out on a planting scheme, prepares a *working plan*. This is a general report on the whole situation; it need not be very elaborate, or very strict in saying what must be done in so many years' time—in fact, the simpler it is the better, provided it doesn't leave out anything essential. As long as it gives an idea of what the forester has in mind when he decides to plant larch here, beech there, and spruce on the far side of the hill, then whoever takes over control of the woods after him will be able to continue on much the same lines.

Actually, a working plan deals with the existing woods as well as the newly planted ones, so that all the woodlands are brought under one plan of management. By this means there grows up a con-tinuous cycle or programme of work: "This year we shall fell 10 acres of Park Wood, thin out the 30-year-old larch in Deadman's Coppice, weed the 8 acres we planted last year, and replant the recently cleared 11 acres in the north-west of Badger's Wood. Next year...." And so it goes on, until the woodlands are brought to the desirable state known as *Normal Forest*, when they will have become divided into equal areas of increasing ages, the youngest just planted and the oldest ripe for the axe. When the oldest has been felled, it will be replanted and become the youngest; and so the cycle continues.

IV. WORK AND THE SEASONS

Willow warbler on
a flowering larch twig

SPRING

NOW that the time has come to discuss how the woodman's work is controlled by the seasons, we are up against rather a problem. To start with spring seems a natural thing to do; yet the woodman's year doesn't really begin in the spring—in fact, it is difficult to say when it does begin; October is as good a dividing line as any. The point is that the forester's work is not related to the months to the same extent as the farmer's. Haytime and harvest, two important periods in the farmer's year, are of limited duration and come at about the same time every year. By way of contrast, planting and felling, two important operations in the woodman's year, are not nearly so urgent. In most cases they can be done any time the tree is resting—or, as they say, when the sap is down (although you've got to choose your weather, and be very wary when there's frost about).

However, there is probably still some planting to be done in the spring, so we'll deal with that first, and forget about felling until the winter.

Planting

When we speak of planting we mean the setting out of young trees already partly developed. There are other methods of establishing woodlands; you can, for example, sow your seeds straightaway in the plantation. This direct sowing is suitable for large seeds like acorns, beech-mast and Spanish chestnuts. On the Continent and elsewhere the commonest method of growing trees in the forest is by "natural regeneration". The area to be renewed is cleared of all but a few healthy "mother" trees which shed their seeds and gradually surround themselves by a large family of youngsters. When this has happened to his satisfaction, the forester cuts down and takes away the mother trees a few at a time until no old trees remain and the whole area is covered by a dense growth of young seedlings. These seedlings are gradually thinned out, the best being left to form the final crop.

A very good idea, you may say, and much more pleasant to look at than rows and rows of trees set up like wooden soldiers. Yes, it is a good method; but it isn't very satisfactory in this country. Some of our native and well-established species, such as oak, beech, syca-more, and birch, are capable of producing good crops of seed only in certain years, and these fruitful years are irregular and often far between. Consequently the more artificial method of planting is adopted in England.

You often hear it asked why foresters will insist on growing acres and acres of conifers, like larch, spruce, and pine, instead of the hardwoods that seem more native to the English countryside. "Look how we are gradually losing our lovely oak and beech woods", they say, "and setting up foreign species which don't fit in with the English landscape." The chief reason for this is that timber buyers require much more softwood than hardwood, and as the forester must satisfy his customers he has little choice in the matter. A hundred and

44

part of the trunk and branch
of an oak growing in the open

fifty years ago oak was in demand, and lots of it, for building ships. And here it is interesting to notice how forestry methods alter. In those days oaks were encouraged to throw out branches as low down as possible, because the ship-builders needed "crooks" for their hulls, which could be cut out of the curved portion formed by the branches and the main stem. To achieve this sort of growth meant that the oaks were spaced some distance apart, with lots of room to themselves, so that the branches could expand freely. But to-day the buyers want good straight timber without branches, so the idea is to grow the trees nearer together. They then become so busy struggling towards the light out of the shade of their neighbours that all their energy and growth goes into the main stem, which is what the merchants want.

We still grow hardwoods, of course, but probably not more than one acre to every five acres of conifers. Compared with the hardwoods, too, softwoods take a shorter time to mature. The best oak is felled when it is something like 100 to 120 years old, but conifers can be felled in sixty to eighty years.

What kind of trees you plant is largely decided by the type of soil you are going to plant them in. Some species are very particular in this respect: for instance, ash needs the richest woodland soil, beech flourishes on chalk or limestone, and some of the pines thrive best on poor, light land.

Let us imagine that it is early spring, and that the woodman is about to do a day's planting. He is lucky in having just the right sort

45

of weather—slightly moist, but warm, and with hardly any wind. He is glad that the frosts are over—for the time being, at any rate—because besides making the ground hard to work they are very dangerous to his young trees. He and his fellows are going to start in the seven-acre plot that was felled last year. It is all ready for them; they have cleared the ground of the rubbish left over from the felling, they have dug a few open drains in the corner where the water used to lie about, and the whole area is fenced against rabbits. They are going to plant larch. It is a good loamy soil here, and they know it will grow because there are some flourishing young larch plantations not far away. The young trees—two year one year transplants—were delivered a couple of days ago; since then they have been in the nursery with their roots buried in the soil. The head woodman carries a painted stick, marked in feet, and a long roll of twine. These are for measuring the distance at which the plants will be set out. As a matter of fact, with *his* experience he could do it just as well by eye; but he's a cautious fellow and doesn't quite trust the others at guesswork.

As the plantation is quite near the nursery, little time will be wasted in moving the plants from one to the other. Each of the men has got a bit of sacking tied round him, bent double to form a pouch—rather like a kangaroo's. In this he carries the plants, so that their roots shall not become dry. He fills his sack in the nursery, and sets off to get the trees in the ground as soon as he can.

And now the head woodman and one of his assistants are in the plantation setting out the lines. They stand on the opposite boundaries and lay the cord down between them. The head man walks along the cord with his measuring rod, and every five feet he puts down one of the young larches. When he has finished the row the cord is moved forward, parallel with its last position and five feet away; this gives the line for the second row.

Meanwhile the other woodmen proceed to plant the young larches

46

where they have been laid. For this they have a special kind of spade, with the sides of the blade tapering to a point, although the more usual type can be used.

Planting spade

Watch how the woodman puts the plants in. He makes a sharp downward cut, prises the spade about a little, and withdraws it. Next, he makes another cut below the first, at right angles to it, rather like the letter T upside down. Without with-drawing the spade from the second cut —the cross-piece of the T—he presses down the handle of the spade towards him, lifting the earth a little so that the first notch gapes open, and into the hole he pops the young tree, being careful to see that its roots are in straight. Finally he releases the pressure and withdraws the spade, allowing the soil as it sinks back to grip the young tree; and with his

Making the "notch"

heel he firms the soil round about it. He can then pass on to the next.

This is a rapid method known as *notch planting*, and on an easy soil an experienced woodman can plant up to about 1000 trees a day, if he is kept constantly supplied. Of course, there are other ways of going about it. The most thorough is called *pit planting*, where a separate hole is dug for each tree; but this is slow and therefore costs more, for a man can plant only about 120 to 150 a day.

A mattock

Then there is *mattock planting*, useful where the ground is rough or stony. The mattock is a double-sided tool rather like a short-bladed pickaxe. One side acts as a strong hoe, while the other is either in the form of a pointed pick or fashioned with an axe edge for cutting through roots. The woodman first clears away any coarse vegetation with the hoe part, then he loosens the soil with the pick, and then he makes a hole with the hoe; he inserts the plant, withdraws the mattock, and finishes off by heeling the soil firm.

The poorer types of soil may call for special systems such as *mound planting*: the woodman digs up a few spadefuls of earth and makes a little mound, which he leaves for some time to let it settle. Later in the season he notches the plant in the centre of the mound.

In a very few days our seven-acre plot will be all planted, and with the hope that it will turn out a success the woodman can go on to something else.

We saw that our head man was setting out his larch five feet apart. Why five feet? you may wonder. Well, the best spacing for each of the various kinds of trees is pretty well known now as the result of experience, as most foresters agree to-day. Once it was the custom to grow trees very close together in the hope that in the struggle for room to live the stronger trees would soon naturally kill off the poorer ones, and thus lessen the need of the forester's care in the future. But this is no longer thought to be a wise plan, for the fewer plants you need grow in an acre from the start the cheaper it will be to establish the plantation.

The closest grown species is beech, which is planted four feet apart in each row, and the rows four feet from each other. This means that in every acre you start off with 2722 seedlings. When you realize that an acre of beechwood ready for felling will consist of only about

48

120 trees, you may reflect that quite a few of the youngsters haven't much life to look forward to. The reason for this close spacing is simply that beech cannot bear much light; if it is left alone in the open it feels very sorry for itself. Beech is known as a *shade-bearing* species, in contrast with, say, larch, which likes a great deal of light. Most trees are light-demanding—in fact, of the commoner kinds, only Silver fir and hornbeam share the beech's love of shade.

Very few trees are planted wider than six feet apart when grown in plantations. Even then, you have to start off with 1210 to the acre. It may seem rather a waste, but it is a great advantage to have a large choice when it comes to selecting your final crop.

The practice of planting in straight lines makes the wood seem very artificial at first, but gradually as the plantations thicken out they begin to look more natural. The blessing of straight lines is that they allow the woodman to move among them more easily for such work as pruning and thinning.

Where a big area is being planted the forester will miss out several consecutive rows at intervals to form *rides*. Rides are clear lanes

A forest ride opening on to a main road

through the woods, and they are useful for timber to be dragged along. For you must remember that at some time in the future the forester will want to cut down his trees, and unless he provides himself in good time with trackways he is going to find great difficulty in hauling them out. Rides are also helpful if a fire breaks out, for an open lane will check the fierceness of the fire and the flames may be unable to jump across to the next block. The wider rides are called *roads*. Where a lot of timber is likely to be hauled across them they are often made up with solid foundations. The rides lead into the roads in a criss-cross pattern, and the forest roads run directly to the public roads, so that in a well-arranged forest there is no difficulty in dragging any of the timber wherever it may be wanted.

Beating-up

When a plantation is first stocked it is unlikely that all the trees will survive the first year or two, and the forester has to go round and fill up the gaps where young trees have died. This is called *beating-up*. We know already that the forester expects a great number of his young trees never to grow up; but it is important that there should be no serious gaps in the pattern in the early days.

Beating-up begins in the first season after planting, and the method is much the same. The woodman takes his planting tool and a supply of transplants, and walks up and down the rows looking for dead trees. When he finds one he pulls it out by the roots and plants another in its place. Sometimes he will economize, where there are several gaps next to each other, by putting in only two where there were three before, and so on.

The following year he may have to go through the plantation again, but once the wood begins to put on height it is not advisable to continue beating-up, because the smaller transplants would only be overshadowed and handicapped by their neighbours.

Beech seedling, showing the long tap-root

Nursery work

Spring is a busy time for lifting the nursery seedlings and lining them out in their new beds. The object of this, as we have seen, is to give the roots more room to develop. For some species, this is especially important: oak and beech, for example—which produce what is called a *tap-root*. This is an extra large root which plunges deep into the ground and forms a sturdy anchor. If you leave such a tree too long, the tap-root gets such a grip that it is difficult to move the tree without hurting it: a tap-rooted tree has fewer root fibres, and therefore needs to be handled respectfully. Provided you lift it early enough, you can safely cut a bit off the tap-root, and when the tree is replanted it will grow many more root fibres than it would if left alone.

Transplanting is a rather more thorough job than planting in the woodlands, because the seedlings are smaller and more delicate; as with all young things, the early stages of life are particularly important. The ground must first be dug over and cleared of weeds, and then a series of trenches is prepared about a foot deep and nine to twelve inches apart. The young plants are lifted from the seed-beds by having the earth below them gently prised up with a fork.

Now comes an important question: Which of the seedlings should be transplanted, and which thrown away? There is always a great variation in their size and quality; some will be strong and well-rooted, others lanky and crooked, others with poor roots, and so on. Obviously it is a waste of time and money to keep the bad specimens, so the woodman takes this opportunity of *culling* and *grading*. One way of doing it is this: supposing he decides to sort them out or grade them in three classes, he spreads out his left hand and tucks the plants between his fingers. Since at one or two years old they are only a few inches long, he can hold quite a lot at a time. He will put the strongest and healthiest class between his first and second fingers, the next class between the second and third fingers, and the weak ones with forked stems, bad roots or other faults between his third and fourth fingers. As he judges the class of a seedling by comparing it with others, this method of keeping them apart and yet ready in his hand makes it easy for him to see at once in which group to place each seedling as he picks it up. If he were to mix them all up in the transplant lines, the chances are that the better ones would get better and the weaker plants weaker than ever; but by putting all the firsts together in the same trenches, and all the seconds together, this handicap is removed. The worst lot—the *culls*, that is—are not

likely to do well anyhow, so the woodman will probably burn them.

While he is handling the seedlings the woodman must see that the roots are not left exposed to the air any longer than can be helped. If he has a lot of grading to do before lining them out in the new trenches, he will have to heel them in the ground for the time being, covering their roots with moist soil.

Their distance apart in the transplant beds depends on the kind of tree; it may be from two to six inches. The nearer together he can put them the less work will

Transplanting into the nursery lines

the woodman have to do, because at three inches he can get twice as many into the same trench as at six. He sets them by placing their roots against the side of the trench, and fixing them in position with a handful of earth. When the whole line is completed the trench can be filled up and the soil gently firmed round the young plants.

Sometimes the job is done by using *planting boards*. These are long planks, hinged in pairs like a portfolio. The seedlings are laid along one of them at regular intervals, with the twigs towards the hinge and the roots overlapping the edge. Then the top board is folded over and fixed in position, so that all you can see is a row of rootlets. The woodman picks the whole thing up, stands it up over the crack of a narrow trench, and gets one of his fellows to fork the earth about the roots. He then unfastens the boards, moves them aside, and— hey presto!—there you have a trim little regiment of transplants, as regular and upright as you please.

After he has lined out his seedlings in their new beds—or possibly before—it doesn't really matter—the woodman may have some older transplants to transplant again. This time he will be dealing with young trees that need a bit more room because they have grown much bigger since they were last lined out. Transplanting a second time will make the roots develop still more, and so the young trees will need to be set farther apart. The method is just the same as before, including the culling of the weaker plants.

It is not always necessary to transplant twice, but a few species seem to benefit—notably, again, those with tap-roots. Sometimes the only reason is that the woodman has more young plants in stock than he needs for the year's planting, but this isn't a very good one. However, I once saw it carried so far that the poor unwanted trees were transplanted five times. In the end they grew so large that the woodman decided not to move them again but to leave them in the nursery to provide shelter!

SUMMER

After a busy winter and spring you might think that the woodman had earned the right to a little rest, a time in which he could take his ease and watch his charges grow. But, unfortunately for him, summer is just the season when his woodlands need protection—against weeds, against insects, against fungi, and against fire.

Weeds are a great problem in the nursery and in the youngest plantations. In older woods the trees are strong enough to master them, but until that time comes the woodman should pay as much attention to the destruction of weeds as the farmer and the gardener.

The hardest work is in the nursery, especially the seed-beds, for here the trees are so small that they would be easily overrun. Whether in the nursery or in the plantation, the danger of unchecked weeds is that they might smother the trees and deprive them of the light, air, and moisture they need. The weeds you find in the nursery are of the garden sort: groundsel, shepherd's purse, bindweed, and others.

Thorough hoeing is the usual way of keeping them in check, so that their roots become exposed and the whole plant can be picked up and put on a bonfire. It is very necessary to burn them, otherwise they will seed themselves and cause further trouble.

In the woods themselves you will find more stubborn kinds of weed. Some of them, such as foxglove, willow herb, heather, and gorse, are so attractive that it seems a pity not to let them grow. Then there are the climbing weeds, like honeysuckle and traveller's joy (often called "old man's beard"). But no woodman could have anything to say in favour of brambles; and gorse too, as you know, is apt to get in the way! Other plants, useful in the right place, are classed as weeds when they interfere with the main crop of trees: for example, blackthorn, holly, and even birch and alder.

The hoe would be of little use for tackling weeds in plantations, so the woodman uses a bill-hook or a sickle. He works his way over the whole area, row by row, cutting down the weeds as near to the ground as possible and pulling them away from the young trees. He has to keep very wide awake all the time, because where the weeds are so thick as to smother the trees it is sometimes difficult to cut through one without the other.

Lately, however, foresters have found out that weeding can be too thorough, and that by leaving some of the weed growth the trees benefit by the shade it affords. They seem to be all the better for a little healthy competition, and don't

Clearing bracken from young trees

55

mind taking up the challenge of the weeds if the weeds are not too strong. Nowadays, therefore, instead of making a clean sweep of all the weeds, a number of them are allowed to remain, to be slowly driven under by the trees themselves. This is quite a good instance of how forestry ideas may and do change as our knowledge grows.

Once the young plantation is reaching the thicket stage—which may be in three or four years time, when even the unobservant can see that there is something inside the wired enclosure after all—weeding becomes unnecessary, apart from an occasional assault upon the climbing parasites, like bindweed and honeysuckle. And later still when you can't, as they say, see the wood for trees, the forest floor becomes so shaded that the weeds give up the battle.

Insects

The warm weather is the time for most of the woodman's insect enemies to sit up and take notice, and the early summer is a busy season for them and for the woodman because of their destructive habits. To understand properly what sort of damage insects do, the woodman needs to know something of their life histories. Most insects go through a series of changes before assuming their mature form. They begin as an egg, which hatches into a grub or caterpillar. Any grub or caterpillar is an insect in the second stage of its strange life; it spends its time feeding and growing, and sometimes as it grows it changes its skin every now and again. After a time of nothing but feeding it turns into a chrysalis (or *pupa*) and gives up feeding altogether, sleeping and changing inside its cocoon. The third stage of the insect's life begins when the chrysalis wakes up and the winged and perfect insect emerges. It is the perfect insect that lays the eggs which will begin the story all over again. Those of you who have kept caterpillars in glass jars or glass-topped boxes will have watched these changes yourselves, unless the caterpillars have escaped, as they generally seem to!

Damage to trees may be caused by insects either as caterpillars or as winged insects. Sometimes the harm is so slight as not to matter; on the other hand, the damage may be bad enough to destroy whole plantations of trees. Those who know most about forest insects group them according to the kind of damage they do. Thus, there are (i) those which feed upon the leaves, (ii) those which bore their way into buds, leaves, shoots, or seeds, (iii) those which feed under the bark, (iv) those which bore into the wood, and (v) those which feed on the roots.

A full list of the insects the woodman may have to combat would be long enough to carry us over the next two seasons, so we had better be content with a few of the commoner species, and see what remedies can be used against them.

The *pine weevil* is as much of a nuisance as any, and you may come across him in conifer woods between May and September. You can distinguish weevils from other kinds of beetle by their long snouts, with club-shaped *antennae* or feelers growing out of the tip. They lay their eggs on the stumps of softwood trees (chiefly pines, spruces, and Douglas fir) which have been felled some little time ago. When the eggs are hatched the weevil-grubs start eating little galleries in the inner

Pine weevils

bark and sapwood of the stumps, and so far they can't be said to be harming anybody. But once they have turned into perfect weevils they feed on the bark of young trees and leave the wood bare underneath, which is then open to other forms of attack. Sometimes the plants are nibbled right round so that there is no more hope for them, and in the very worst cases the bark may be all chewed off.

The woodman can do much to *prevent* an attack by removing old stumps and burning the rubbish round about; but if the weevils have already appeared he has to think of something else. One remedy is to go round collecting them off the plants. As this is too much to do alone he gets others to help him; I have seen a gang of fifteen children or so weevil hunting. They moved steadily through the wood, collecting them in tins and boxes, and although they got paid for it they seemed to be enjoying themselves so much that I believe they would have done it for nothing.

Another remedy is to set traps for the weevils: these are simply sticks of pinewood with the bark stripped off. They are stuck in the ground at intervals, in the month of June; the weevils lay their eggs in them, and three or four months later the woodman pulls the traps out and burns them. Or he may scatter squares of bark face downwards on the ground. The weevils collect underneath for a gossip and a bit of sleep, and just when they're congratulating themselves on a fine, warm shelter the avenging woodman swoops on them!

The *pine beetle* is much smaller than the weevil, being less than a quarter of an inch long, but he is just as common and just as much of a nuisance. The eggs are laid in the stumps of felled pines, or in sickly trees, and hatch out in April or May. The beetles appear in June or July, and feed on young pine shoots by boring into the pith and eating their way along. The result is that the shoots are hollowed out, and when a strong wind comes they are blown off the tree. Next time you see a pine tree surrounded by fallen clumps of needles, pick up one of the shoots and split it up with your finger nail. You'll probably see a tunnel inside, and there may be a pine beetle lurking at one end.

The *cockchafer* is a well-known insect, with its reddish brown coat of armour plating, and its habit of suddenly crashing into you in the fading light of a summer evening. Although it feeds on the leaves of the oak and

Cockchafer grub

"We have to rely on birds"

other broad-leaved trees, it doesn't really do much harm to them; in fact, it wouldn't be so unpopular if it hadn't been such a nuisance when a grub. The grubs hatch out underground in the summer, and live in the soil for three or four years before turning into their chrysalis form. During that long time they feed on the roots of any kind of tree that happens to be near at hand, very often killing young plants in the process. The cockchafer grub is most troublesome in the nursery, because it thrives best in freshly dug soil and can there get at an unlimited number of the youngest, juiciest roots. There isn't much the woodman can do except to collect and destroy every grub he finds whenever the nursery ground is being dug. They are easy to see; for they are big and of a whitish colour.

A pest of a different kind is the *oak-leaf roller moth*, a little grey-green creature with a wing span of about an inch. In seasons favourable to themselves they appear in swarms in oak woods during the early summer. The caterpillars are the villains of the piece, because they feed on the young leaves, and where there are large numbers of them whole trees may be stripped bare. It is quite a common sight to see them hanging on threads from the oaks, and if you pass without thinking about them your hat and clothes brush them off as you go along, which means that during the next half mile or so you have to brush them off your clothes! In early June the caterpillars roll a leaf round themselves like a blanket, and go to their chrysalis sleep comfortably inside; and that, of course, is the reason they are called leaf-rollers.

There is no means known of destroying the caterpillars in large numbers, so we have to rely on birds and bad weather to do the job for us.

Fire!

The woodman may be called on to fight a fire at any time of the year, but summer and spring are particularly dangerous seasons. The vegetation then becomes dry and easily inflammable; also, there are

more people about in the country, far too many of whom are very careless about lighting wayside fires or throwing away burning cigarette ends. These are common causes of forest fires, and the public is being constantly asked to be careful of such things. One cigarette stub can cause the loss of acres and acres of woodland. And once a fire takes hold in a wood it is very difficult to put out.

As with everything else, there are right and wrong ways of tackling fires once they have started, but the great thing is to prevent their spreading. We have seen that when plantations are set out it is usual to leave roads and rides at intervals; in some cases the woodman may have to rely on these to check the flames. Fires in pine woods are the most difficult to cope with, but if occasional belts of hardwood trees have been included in the planting there is a chance that a fire will stop short on reaching them; for the foliage of some hardwoods, such as beech and alder, fortunately doesn't burn very easily.

In a spell of dry weather the woodman must be extra vigilant, so that he can see a fire as soon as it starts up. The Forestry Commission build look-out towers in the middle of their large forests from which a watch can be kept over great distances. If the watchman spies anything burning he communicates at once with his fellows, who make for the spot as fast as they can, bringing axes, shovels, firebrooms and anything else that may come in handy.

In fighting a fire the experienced forester splits his men into two gangs on opposite sides of the burning area. Their object is to meet in the middle as soon as they can, beating down the flames as they go with spades and brooms. If there is any wind it is hopeless trying to attack from the front, because of the heat and the smoke. Should the gangs be unable to reduce the width of the burning patch, the most they can do is to prevent it getting any wider, in the hope that the fire will soon come to a ride or open space where it will burn itself out.

When a fire becomes really serious the head woodman may have to order his men to start counter-firing. It is a sad decision for him to make, for it means sacrificing still more of his woods, and he only makes it when nothing else will help. The principle of counter-firing is to steal a march on the fire. By noting which way the fire is coming—and if there is any wind it isn't hard to tell—the woodman and his gang can choose some convenient line a little way ahead where it should be possible to check the flames. A ride is the best sort of line, or perhaps a stream or some natural opening. The men stand

61

with their backs to this line, facing the oncoming fire; then, stepping a few paces forward, each starts another fire of his own. He must concentrate on his private bonfire so that no sparks cross the agreed boundary line; if they do, he jumps on them before they get too big a hold. By the time the big fire turns up it is confronted by a blackened belt with little left to burn upon it. Furthermore, it sets up a draught which sucks the little fires towards it. At last, if the counter-firing has been properly done, the whole thing dies out because there is nothing more to be got at.

It is often difficult to decide whether a fire really has gone out or not. Sometimes the woodman will leave a heap of ashes, convinced that they are dead; yet, when he comes back an hour or a day later he finds them with a new lease of life. The best fires delight in such practical joking!

Thinning

We already know that in the beginning a plantation contains many more trees than will ever come to maturity. Some of them die and are not replaced, but many more are removed by what is called *thinning*.

Thinning does away with the unhealthy trees and gives more room to the rest; it gradually strengthens the others against wind damage; and it brings in money to the forester, because there is a sale for good thinnings. But the main object is the encouragement of the final crop.

You might think it an easy matter to choose which trees should be cut out; there are always a number of scallywags which clearly can come to no good, and others which are taking up too much room with their spreading branches, and so on. But it can be very difficult, especially where you have a plot of similar stems, all of apparently equal growth and equal merit. Some of them have got to come out, otherwise they will all suffer in time when their demand for living room grows more insistent.

However, there is generally a good reason why this or that one should be cut down, and the trained forester can soon make up his mind about it.

Before a tree is touched by the axe the forester walks through the whole plantation, or a large portion of it, marking those which are to come out. In this way he can form an idea of what the whole will look like when the thinning is done. If he were merely to go round lopping down a tree here and one there in piecemeal fashion he might find that he had taken out too many or left an uneven stand.

The marking is done with a *scribe*, which makes a scratch by cutting a narrow slice in the bark. If the strange people who like carving their names on trees were to use one of these it would take very much less of their time than a penknife! The forester decides which trees are to be taken out as he walks through the wood, and makes a X or some such mark on each.

A double-mark scribe with knuckle-guard

It is best to mark too few at first, rather than too many; if you haven't taken out enough you can always go through the wood again and put that right; but if you have cut down too many it's no good trying to put them back!

Soon after the marking has been done, the woodman begins to cut the trees. When they are small he likes to use a bill-hook, which doesn't need room for a long swing as the axe does, and is better in a dense plantation. As each tree is cut he cleans it by trimming the crown and knocking off the side branches. The poles are then taken to the nearest ride and stacked ready for removal by the timber waggon. They are easy to drag out because they are young and slender, and it doesn't take the woodman long to fell, trim, and stack each pole.

How many stems does the woodman remove at a thinning? That depends on many things: the kind of tree, the age of the plantation, and the rate at which it has grown. During the course of its life a wood will be reduced gradually by several thinnings; if the woodman thought to save himself trouble by having one glorious clear-up and no more he would find that the remaining stems would take advantage of the enormous increase in light and room by branching wide and all over the place. The prudent forester has a maxim, *Thin lightly, thin little, thin often*. Here is an example showing how judicious thinning affects the number of trees in a wood.

An acre plot is planted with European larch, put in five and a half feet apart. This means there are 1440 trees to the acre. The first thinning, when the plantation is twelve years old, will take out perhaps 220. In another three years some 130 more will be removed. The third thinning may take place at twenty years, when 150 or so will be cut. After this the woodman will gently thin the plantation about every five years, taking out a smaller number each time. When the trees are thirty-five years old over half their number will have gone; at sixty years there will be less than 300 still standing; and the final crop, at sixty-five years or thereabouts, will comprise perhaps 230 mature trees.

Don't, by the way, regard this as a hard and fast subtraction table. There is so much variation in the growth of every forest crop that it would be a waste of time to lay down laws about thinning. It is an art acquired by practice, which reading alone can't teach—still, doesn't this apply to every art?

Brashing

This sounds like a home-made word, but whatever the origin it's really rather descriptive. It means going through a young plantation and generally cleaning it up; "brushing up" is another expression used in the same sense. You can imagine that when a wood begins to grow, a lot of the lower branches die off for want of air and sunlight, and tend to clutter up the place so that it is difficult to move

Brashing

among the rows to see what is going on inside. When the woodman wants to mark the trees for thinning he must be able to get a general view of the stems and the canopy; therefore, some time beforehand he arms himself with his trusty old bill-hook and disappears into the thicket. Some trees lend themselves very easily to brashing —with larch, for example, the lower branches die quickly and thoroughly, and all the woodman has to do is to knock them off near the stem with the back of the bill-hook. It's a pleasure to brash larch; they give such a satisfying crackle even if you strike the branches off with nothing more than your fist. Other species, like Douglas fir, put up more of a fight. The sharp edge of the bill-hook has to be used on them, because the lower branches are very persistent. If the woodman isn't careful he may damage the stems by cutting the branches too deeply into the tree, so that a wound is formed which may never heal.

It is usual to brush up a plantation at least a year before it is thinned to give the rubbish left upon the ground time to rot and settle down. Otherwise the woodman's eyes might be watching the ground for fear he should trip up in the tangle of branches, instead of in the air inspecting the canopy!

*Red squirrel on
a hazel branch*

AUTUMN

With the falling of the leaf the trees let down their sap and prepare
for a long spell of inactivity. And then the woodman can start
thinking of felling and planting. He may still have some thinning to
do, but apart from that his summer tasks are over; it is time to
prepare for the year's planting.

There is much to be done before the young trees can be planted
—how much depending on the state of the ground. If a clearing
felled last year is to be replanted it will probably be full of weeds;
there may be odd branches lying about, rabbits may have settled
themselves in, and the whole place may well have become a wilder-
ness. It will need to be cleaned up, fenced, and possibly drained.

The process of clearing is a combination of cutting all the weeds
with scythes and sickles, and collecting any lop and top left by the
last timber fellers. All the rubbish is assembled in a convenient place
and burned, and if the area still isn't as clean as a farmer would like

66

it—well, we're not sowing wheat, after all! Draining is not often necessary in woodlands, which is just as well because of the expense; but if any portions of the land are waterlogged it is advisable to dig a few trenches on the slope to take the water away. Few trees will flourish where there is moisture lying around their roots; the water gets stagnant and the root-hairs of the plants are unable to absorb it, especially as air cannot circulate there.

Fencing

If you could make a collection of all the harsh things that woodmen throughout the country have said about the rabbit, and add to it all that the farmers have said on the same subject, you would wonder why the timid little creature didn't die of misery! But it is a fact that he is responsible for untold damage to crops and to young trees. It is mainly on his account that the forester has to spend pounds and pounds on setting fences round his plantations. There is hardly a district where the forester dare leave his young trees unprotected by wire netting, for in a short time their stems would be nibbled by rabbits, and their chances of growing normally completely ruined. There are other animals the forester has to guard against: squirrels and mice are a pest in the nursery; and in some parts of the country deer are a great nuisance—and deer-proof fencing is far more elaborate and expensive than rabbit wiring.

Fencing is put up at the very beginning, before the first transplant is set; and when the plantation is completely encircled the woodman must make sure that he hasn't enclosed any rabbits, which thus couldn't get away even if they wanted to. Rough stakes, four or five feet high, are driven in the ground ten or twelve feet apart, with occasionally an extra strong stake doubly secured by a wire brace and peg. Then a single wire strand is fastened along them about three feet from the ground, sometimes plain, sometimes barbed.

Barbed wire is useful for keeping out trespassers as well as smaller game! The netting is bought in rolls of fifty feet; it is commonly three and a half feet high and one and a quarter inch gauge—that is to say, the holes are not more than one and a quarter inches across. This is fastened to the wire strand and fixed down the stakes with staples, the lower six inches being either buried in the ground or turned outwards and laid flat with pegs or sods to anchor it to the soil, so that if rabbits attempt to burrow underneath the fence they are stopped short by a wall of netting.

The pest

In spite of all this rabbits do manage to get into the forbidden area at times, and once in it isn't easy to destroy them. The young trees and undergrowth all offer them ample hiding places, and in large enclosures they can play hide-and-seek to their hearts' content—until they're caught, that is. And this reminds me of a very ingenious trap I was once shown. It comprised a sort of hut made of wire netting with a narrow entrance blocked by a see-saw. This was weighted on the outside, and led directly into the wire hut, which was baited with all kinds of vegetable delicacies. To get at the bait the rabbit had to walk the plank, but it wasn't sufficiently steep or dangerous-looking to deter any other than the most faint-hearted. So the victim walked up the gentle slope which tipped up when he was well inside, and as he jumped or fell off the plank dropped back, out of his reach and ready for the next venturer. The inventor of this device told me that sometimes he found seven or eight rabbits inside when he visited it first thing in the morning. But one day, he said, a friend of his put up a little notice by the see-saw saying "This way in"—and nothing went near it for days afterwards!

The fencing is usually left round the plantation for ten years or more. By that time the trees will have grown a tough bark which is not nearly so palatable to the rabbit as the young stem, and the danger period is over.

Pruning

Young forest trees are often improved by being pruned. Pruning means the removal of the lower branches, which, if they were allowed to remain, would form knots in the timber of the main stem. Foresters still argue among themselves as to how much pruning (if any at all) should be done. Some people believe that if the woods are thick enough at the beginning, the lower branches will prune themselves by dying off for want of light and air. But several species (such as Douglas fir, the spruces, and some of the pines) produce very hardy side branches which are reluctant to die. So to prune or not to prune may depend as much on the manner of the trees' growth as on the personal wish of the woodman.

Pruning must be done while the trees are still young. The smaller the branches that have to be cut away, the smaller will be the scar remaining. It is unnecessary to prune every tree in a plantation; most of them will not be worth the time and expense entailed. Any special treatment like this means extra work, and if it has no effect on the quality of the timber in the tree, it is a waste of money. Therefore it is wisest to choose about 200 or 250 of the best stems per acre and give them constant and careful attention. They should be chosen so that they are as evenly spaced as possible, for if they are going to be among the last to be cut they ought to form a regular stand.

The height to which a tree is pruned will be something like fifteen

Bill-hook

to twenty feet, but no wise woodman will do the job all at once. To prune out so much at one time would mean cutting too much into the crown, and would give the tree such a shock that it might die of its wounds. It is better tackled a bit at a time, with intervals of a few years between each pruning. The first time it will be merely a matter of brashing up the stems to the height the woodman can comfortably reach. Often this is done with a bill-hook, using the back of the tool for the dead branches which snap off easily, and the cutting edge for the rest. Or a saw may be used to give a cleaner finish.

For pruning higher, when the lowest branches are now out of reach of the woodman standing on the ground, he can either carry a light ladder and climb up to do his sawing, or use a special kind of saw set on the end of a pole.

Pit-props stacked at the side of a ride

Pit-props

The sale of timber for pit-props has lately become an important market for foresters. In your walks in wooded country you may have noticed stacks of poles of equal sizes, neatly sawn and trimmed, and set up by the side of a ride. These are pit-props, and they are needed in enormous quantities for supporting tunnels in coal mines. Until recently mine owners imported what they wanted from the

70

Northern European forests, but even before the war a gradual shortage in the amount available from abroad caused the collieries to call upon our home resources.

A great advantage of pit-props is that they can be made out of young trees, which means that the owner doesn't have to wait a lifetime before he can sell his crop. Good thinnings make excellent pit-props. The forester selects and marks the trees as though he were thinning a plantation in the usual way. Instead of an axe, it is better to use a saw to cut the trees down as near ground level as possible, because each extra inch means a bit more usable timber. Next, the poles are shorn of their branches with an axe, and the bark is peeled with a special kind of spade having a sharp edge. The woodman has to aim at a smooth finish, so all snags and splinters need to be shaved clean away.

Now the poles are piled up for several weeks to allow the sap to dry out. Careful stacking makes a big difference to the length of time they take to season. They are laid side by side with perhaps twenty in a row, the bottom row being kept clear of the ground away from the damp. The next row is laid across the first at right angles to it, the third at right angles to the second, and therefore parallel to the first, and so the stack is built up to a convenient height.

When the poles are seasoned—which may take from six weeks to several months—they are cross-cut into lengths, the length depending on the thickness of the poles. For example, a prop which has a diameter of 5 inches at the top should be 5 feet long. Different collieries, however, may have different requirements, so it is unwise to generalize. The cuts must be accurately made at right angles, and there are several kinds of saws specially made for this work.

Timber measuring

Before the forester and the timber merchant come to an arrangement over the sale of certain timber they naturally both want to
know how much is being sold before they agree on a price. Timber
is sold at so much per cubic foot, depending on the species and
quality. The price varies greatly and may be the cause of much
haggling between buyer and seller. The most usual way of valuing
a crop is to measure the trees while they are standing. Many
foresters and timber merchants can go up to any tree, cast an eye
over it, and tell you that it contains (say) forty cubic feet of saleable
timber, or however much it may be—and their estimates are very
near the truth. But the more cautious, who like to make sure, get to
work with a tape measure and a long pole, and work out the result
by arithmetic.

The forester and the timber merchant may value the timber
separately and at their own convenience, or they may do so together,
which is generally the better plan. Opinions often differ as to how
much of a tree ought to be classed as saleable, and much time is
saved if the two parties can argue it out on the spot.

Behold them, then, making for the wood on a mild autumn
morning (let us hope it is mild: there are days when it is almost too
cold to hold a pencil, and others when you get a shower-bath every
time you look up to find the height of a tree!) each with a notebook
and a book of timber tables, and accompanied by an assistant who
brings the tape and the pole.

The tape is specially marked for tree-measuring, and the number
read off on the tape when it is stretched round the trunk will give,
not the full girth but one-quarter of the girth of the tree in inches.
In working out the number of cubic feet of timber in a tree it is
necessary to know the height and the quarter-girth half-way up the
stem.

72

The assistant throws his tape round the first stem, pulls it tight, making sure it is horizontal, and shouts, "Thirteen-and-a-half". Then he sets the pole against the tree while the forester and the timber merchant walk round it to see whether the tree is thoroughly sound. Then:

"Eleven and a half?" says the merchant, meaning the quarter-girth half-way up the stem.

The forester nods.

"Twenty-three?"

"I was going to say twenty-four."

"Twenty-four it is, then," says the merchant (but he won't give way as easily as that every time!)—and twenty-four feet is booked as the height.

And so to the next, a fine oak. "Twenty-one", shouts the assistant, having nearly split himself trying to get the tape round.

"Height: Thirty-two?" suggests the forester.

"Oh, just hark at him!" cries the merchant with assumed indignation: "Twenty-eight. It doesn't go an inch more."

"But what about that big branch on the left. You'll get a lot out of that."

"All right", concedes the timber merchant; "we'll call it twenty-eight and add five cubic feet for the big limb."

And so the day passes, until the last tree is measured and the assistant has scratched the bark with his scribe, as he has done to all the others.

It remains to work out the volume (that is, the number of cubic feet) of timber from the agreed figures. This is a matter of squaring the quarter-girth and multiplying it by the height. Fortunately the forester can spare himself the trouble of working out a tiresome sum for every entry by making use of a book of Timber Tables, a special sort of ready reckoner, which does most of the work for him.

When the two men have agreed together about the volume of timber to be sold (the price per cubic foot they will have haggled over already) the bargain can be sealed. If the amount is large they will also draw up an agreement saying when the money is to be paid over, how much time the purchaser is allowed for felling and removing the trees, what rights of way he can drag the timber along, and so on.

It is not always necessary to measure every single tree to be sold. This is the wisest plan when only certain selected trees are being cut down; but where a big area is to be clear felled both parties may be content to work out the value of a whole wood on a system of averages—measuring a plot here and another there. As long as these plots really are "average", that is, representative of the wood as a whole, the result will be much the same.

WINTER

In the half-light of a cold December morning you may say that the woodman is little to be envied, but with so much to be done during the winter he has every chance of keeping warm. Apart from work in the woods, the nursery needs a good deal of attention. One of the most important winter jobs is sowing the seed-beds; this comes towards the end of the season.

But before the seeds are planted the soil must be finely cultivated by digging, weed collecting, and raking. Frost is a great ally because it causes the clods to break down into fine particles. The farmer benefits by frost in the same way; he leaves his fields full of large clods after the autumn ploughing, and when the moisture inside them freezes it expands with a shattering effect.

There are two ways of sowing seeds in the nursery, broadcasting and drilling. In broadcasting the bed is made level with a toothless rake and the seed is scattered all over the place by hand. In drilling very narrow, shallow trenches are made by pressing a board into the soil in parallel lines a few inches apart, and sprinkling the seeds evenly along the trenches. In either method the seeds are afterwards covered either by drawing a thin layer of soil over them, or by sprinkling fine sand on top. After one growing season there should be a thick crop of seedlings.

But seeds have their enemies. Birds, mice, frost, and strong sunlight are all liable to hurt them, as well as certain insects and fungi. As a precaution against mice it is quite common to treat the seeds before sowing with a preparation of red lead, which spoils the flavour for the mice. And, of course, mouse-traps are useful things to have about. Birds are kept away by hanging string nets over the beds, in the gardener's fashion.

Strong sunshine is hardly to be feared in winter, but a simple device for protection against both frost and sun is often used, and the woodman attends to it as soon as the seeds are planted. Wooden pegs, a foot or so long, are stuck into the ground at the corners of the beds, and wire or webbing is stretched across them to form a frame. A covering is then made by fastening strips of wood, such as builders' laths, to two strips of webbing, rather like Venetian blinds. These are laid across the frames to act as a shade for the beds; and they can be rolled up into compact bundles when they are not wanted. In severe frost further protection is given by laying straw, or pine or spruce branches, on top of these coverings.

Felling

A good deal of forethought, as well as physical effort, goes into the felling of a tree. Of course, it becomes second nature to a capable forester; he can tell exactly how and where to make it fall so that it

shall not damage itself or the other trees—or, one might add, the woodmen themselves.

The most usual way of felling big timber is to cut through the trunk just above ground with the axe and the saw. It is possible to grub up the soil surrounding the base of the trunk and sever the exposed roots, but this is a long and tiresome business. No one can watch a woodman at work without marvelling at his accuracy in making the tree fall just where he wants it. He begins by "setting-in" a wedge-shaped cut with the axe; this cut is made on the side towards which the tree is to come down, and near the ground so as to waste as little timber as possible out of the stem. When the axe has well bitten in, the woodman takes his double-handed saw and with his mate prepares to cut through the stem *from the opposite side*. This sawing is pretty hard work. The men kneel down to the job and seem to fall at once into a machine-like rhythm, swinging their bodies from the hips while the saw slowly bites farther and farther into the wood. If you have ever tried your hand at it, just for the fun of the thing, you must have wondered how any human being can keep it up for so long as the woodman does.

77

As the saw nears the centre of the tree the weight of the wood above it may grip the saw and make it jam, and to relieve the pressure the woodman drives one or two wedges into the saw cut with a mallet. These wedges are about six inches long, made of iron, and they do much to ease the labour.

By and by the tree gives a warning creak. The cutters pause, looking upwards for signs of movement. Then, if nothing more happens, they continue to saw—perhaps a little more cautiously. At length the tree begins to tremble, as though undecided; then slowly it starts to fall, and the end has come. It is a moving sight, that final collapse: the unwilling, uncertain beginning, the quickly gathering speed of the fall, and the loud slow crash as the tree meets the ground and its branches crumple under the blow.

And now it is down, it remains for the woodman to clean up the stem, sawing off the side branches and the crown (the "lop and top") to produce a shorn stem ready to be taken to the timber yard. There may sometimes be useful wood in the crown, substantial side branches which can be separately trimmed and converted into quite big planks; but more often the lop and top is of little value, and it may be barely worth the cost of sawing, stacking and removal. Still, it can always be used for firewood; the thinnest branches may be bound into faggots, and probably the bigger stuff will yield fencing-stakes.

Hauling

The great log has now to be taken from the wood to the timber yard, and very awkward it may prove to be. The first step is to get it to a ride where it can be loaded on to a waggon. This is done by fixing a chain round the butt end (the largest end) and getting a horse or a tractor to drag it out of the wood. It needs much skill to move so cumbersome a burden without causing damage to other trees, but most foresters are expert at such manœuvres.

There are several ways of loading the trunks. Sometimes thick poles and chains are built up on the spot into a sort of crane; or, again, balks (or rough beams) of timber may be sloped from the ground to the floor of the waggon, and the stems rolled up by levers. How the difficulty of lifting the heavy log is overcome depends upon what tools are handy, and the foreman's ingenuity in using them. One type of carrier deserves special mention, the "timber-bob" or "janker". It consists of two broad wheels, five or six feet in diameter, connected by a curved iron axle to which is fixed a strong shaft with an iron hook at the shorter end.

The janker is wheeled over the log to be carried, around the middle of which a chain has been fastened; the long end of the shaft is raised and the iron hook at the other end is hooked into the chain. By drawing down the long end of the shaft the log is lifted clear of the ground; and the long arm of the shaft is then held down by being fastened to the other end of the log. If the log has been well balanced the janker and its load can be dragged on the wheels without much effort.

And when the year's timber is felled and carted the woodman turns to planting once again. . . .